Dangerous Animals

Steve Pollock

BBC Children's Books

Hello! I'm Stinky the skunk from *The Animal Show*, and Jake the polar bear and I are going to look at dangerous animals. We have had some really dangerous guests on the show, but none of them have frightened us, have they, Jake?

Stinky, the way you skunks smell when you get scared, nobody wants to upset you! Anyway, let's ask some of our dangerous friends to introduce themselves.

Hello, I'm Achilles the shark. Sharks can swim very fast and some of us eat almost anything, so other fish have to watch out when we're around.

I'm Victor the rattlesnake and I try my best to tell everyone I am around when I rattle my tail. If you listen for me and keep out of my way, I won't hurt you.

I'm a crocodile and I'm Sly by name and sly by nature. Keep away from me when I'm hungry!

△ *Lioness and kill*

Why are some animals more dangerous than others, Jake?

It's because some animals are *predators*. This means that they have to kill another animal to get their next meal. The animals they kill are called *prey*. This lioness has killed an antelope. If she could not kill she would starve to death.

Take a closer look at the face of a tiger and you can see why it is a dangerous animal. The long, sharp teeth are for piercing and tearing. The tiger is such a strong and powerful animal that it can even kill an animal bigger than itself.

▽ *Tiger snarling*

We lions and leopards are both dangerous. We are predators too, and we hunt animals such as antelopes, wild pigs or zebras.

Male lions like me live with other female lions in a group which is called a *pride*. The lionesses in the pride hunt together, running after their prey, and then we all share the food between us. Lions are very strong and we can kill large animals like buffaloes because we hunt in groups.

▽ *Male lion*

△ *Leopard*

The leopard hunts by ambushing its prey. It usually kills smaller animals because it hunts on its own and it does not have to share its food with others. Leopards are very strong animals and can lift a kill into a tree. But big cats like us don't kill the animals we prey on just for fun. We only hunt and kill when we're hungry, so we're not dangerous all the time.

◁ *Polar bear*

Some dangerous animals look rather cuddly. But polar bears can be very dangerous because we prey on seals and other animals for food. It is very cold in the Arctic where we live, and a polar bear needs to eat a lot of food to stay warm. If you get too close to one, you might become its lunch! Don't worry, Stinky, I'm friendly.

This cheetah looks so friendly that you could stroke it, but trying to stroke a wild animal would upset it. If it got upset and thought you were attacking it, it might fight back. Although cheetahs kill other animals for food, they would rather run away than fight another fierce animal.

▷ Cheetah

◁ *Brown bear snarling*

How can I tell if an animal is dangerous, Jake?

Well Stinky, what would you do if this brown bear came near you? Shake it by the paw and say "Hi, my name's Stinky," or run away?

I suppose he does look rather dangerous, Jake. He is certainly letting you know how he feels.

Western diamondback rattlesnake △

Rattlesnakes make a very loud noise by shaking the rattle at the end of their tails. Snakes are actually deaf, so they cannot hear the noise they make. They shake their rattles to scare off animals that might hurt them by treading on them. They are warning other animals, "Keep away, I am dangerous. I might bite you with my poisonous bite."

Animals warn you they can be dangerous in lots of different ways. The coral snake has bright colours on its body to warn other animals that it is dangerous. Bees and wasps have black and yellow stripes to warn other animals about their poisonous stings.

▽ *Coral snake*

Arrow poison frog ▷

I'm not a dangerous frog, but arrow poison frogs like the one in this picture are brightly coloured to warn other animals that they *are* dangerous. They have a poisonous slimy skin. Arrow poison frogs get their name because native Indians in South and Central America tip their arrows with poison from the skin of these frogs.

Black widow spider △

As you can see, not all dangerous animals have to be big and fierce. There are some quite small ones that are dangerous too. Some of the most dangerous animals in the world are poisonous spiders. Which of these do you think is the most dangerous?

Funnel web spider ▷

Actually, the most dangerous types are funnel web spiders from Australia and female black widow spiders from North America.

They both have such strong poison that they could even kill a person, but don't worry, they'd rather keep out of your way! The hairy spider is a bird-eating spider and although it is much bigger than the other two it is much less dangerous.

◁ *Bird-eating spider*

Is it only animals that prey on other animals or that have poison which are dangerous?

Well Stinky, some animals are dangerous even though they only eat plants. They attack to protect themselves if they feel threatened.

The African buffalo is like a huge bull. If people disturb a buffalo it might chase them if it thinks it is being attacked. Buffaloes are heavy and very strong. They have huge horns which can even hurt attacking lions.

▽ *African buffalo*

△ **Hippopotamus**

The hippopotamus eats grass and other plants. But with such big teeth and its large size, a hippopotamus can be quite dangerous, particularly to people. The hippo's big front teeth are normally used for fighting other hippos. But if a hippo felt threatened, it might attack a person.

△ *Hammerhead sharks*

Everyone knows that sharks can be dangerous, but only some kinds such as these hammerhead sharks have been known to attack people. Other kinds, like the great white shark, are dangerous too. They are very big and they eat just about anything. A great white shark can grow as long as three grown up people. One great white shark was found with an old boot, a plastic bucket, a bottle of wine and a big solid iron moneybox in its stomach!

This reef shark shows how the sharp, slim shape of a shark's body helps it swim quickly through the water. Sharks do not have good eyesight but they can smell the blood of other animals from well over a mile away, and they can swim faster than a lot of other sea creatures. Like many dangerous animals, sharks have lots of teeth for gripping their prey, but instead of chewing their food they bolt it down in large chunks. They don't have any table manners, do they?

▽ *Reef shark*

△ *Crocodiles on a river bank*

Well Stinky, would you ever smile at a crocodile?

I'd rather not, Jake. I know they are dangerous!

We crocodiles are just doing our job, like any other dangerous animal. We lie hidden in the water and sneak up on animals as they come for a drink. We grab them by the snout and pull them into the water to drown. We might even do that to a person, if they came too near!

△ *Crocodile's mouth*

Can you see that great big mouth full of teeth? Crocodiles' teeth drop out all the time but there are always new ones growing. So we always have a mouth full of teeth. I have such a powerful bite that it would be difficult for any animal caught in my mouth to escape. But you can keep the mouth of a crocodile closed with one hand. Do you want to have a go, Stinky?

No thanks, Sly!

Well Jake, I have never seen so many scary animals in one go. And I don't want to see many more. I just can't get used to the idea that any one of these could really hurt me or even eat me.

You have to understand that just because they are dangerous doesn't mean these animals are going to be dangerous to *you*. If you stay out of their way, they will probably not hurt you. Most animals that live in the wild live among dangerous animals. Even dangerous animals like these buffaloes will be in danger from lions wanting to hunt them. That is because hunting and killing is a way of life for many animals. You have nothing to worry about, Stinky; all those animals will stay away from you because of your nasty smell!

Thanks, Jake. Now I know why I like my smell so much!

△ Herd of buffaloes

Running lioness ▽

Picture Credits

All wildlife photographs supplied by **Oxford Scientific Films** and credited to: **Animals Animals** pages 10 (Tom Edwards), 13 (Zig Leszczynski), 14 (Breck P. Kent), 17 (Henry Ausloos) and 21 (Zig Leszczynski); **Martin Chillmaid** page 15 (bottom); **Bruce Davidson** page 16; **Mark Deeble and Victoria Stone** page 7; **Michael Fogden** page 12; **Dan Guravich** page 8; **Howard Hall** page 18; **Mantis Wildlife** page 15 (top); **Stan Osolinski** page 20; **Photo Researchers** page 6 (Renée Lynn); **Norbert Rosing** page 23 (top); **Survival** front cover and pages 5 (Vivek Sinha), 4 (R. L. Matthews), 9 (Mary Plage) and 19 (Daniel Wills); **Steve Turner** page 23 (bottom); **Tom Ulrich** page 11.

Published by BBC Children's Books
a division of BBC Worldwide Publishing
a subsidiary of BBC Worldwide Limited
Woodlands, 80 Wood Lane, London W12 0TT

First published 1996
Text and design copyright © BBC Children's Books 1996
Based on the television series *Jim Henson's Animal Show* copyright © Jim Henson Productions, Inc. 1996
Muppet character photos and illustrations copyright © 1996 Jim Henson Productions, Inc.
Jim Henson's Animal Show with Stinky and Jake logo and character names and likenesses
are trademarks of Jim Henson Productions, Inc. All rights reserved.

ISBN 0 563 40454 X

Typeset by BBC Children's Books
Cover printed by Clays Ltd, St Ives plc
Colour separations by DOT Gradations, Chelmsford
Printed and bound in Great Britain by Cambus Litho, East Kilbride